Understanding Anxiety

WHAT IS A PANIC ATTACK?

Caitie McAneney

PowerKiDS press

New York

Published in 2021 by The Rosen Publishing Group, Inc.
29 East 21st Street, New York, NY 10010

Copyright © 2021 by The Rosen Publishing Group, Inc.

All rights reserved. No part of this book may be reproduced in any form without permission in writing from the publisher, except by a reviewer.

First Edition

Editor: Kristen Susienka
Book Design: Rachel Rising

Photo Credits: Cover, Pixel-Shot/Shutterstock.com; Cover, NuPenDekDee/Shutterstock.com; Cover, giedre vaitekune/Shutterstock.com; Cover Dejan Dundjerski/Shutterstock.com; Cover, pp.1,3,4,6,8,10,12,14,16,18,20,22,23,24 (background) Flas100/Shutterstock.com; Cover, pp.1,5,7,9,11,13,14,15,17,19,21 (text box) mhatzapa/Shutterstock.com; p. 4 Pete Pahham/Shutterstock.com; p. 5 Song_about_summer/Shutterstock.com; p. 6 Marian Fil/Shutterstock.com; p. 7 Diego Cervo/Shutterstock.com; p. 8 PitukTV/Shutterstock.com; p. 9 Esteban De Armas/Shutterstock.com; p. 10 B-D-S Piotr Marcinski/Shutterstock.com; p. 11 Sabphoto/Shutterstock.com; p. 12 Sebastian Kaulitzki/Shutterstock.com; p. 13 Monkey Business Images/Shutterstock.com; p. 15 Potstock/Shutterstock.com; p. 16 Rae Anna/Shutterstock.com; p. 17 wavebreakmedia/Shutterstock.com; p. 18 se media/Shutterstock.com; p. 19 Photobac/Shutterstock.com; p. 20 Jelena Aloskina/Shutterstock.com; p. 21 New Africa/Shutterstock.com; p. 22 Deman/Shutterstock.com.

Some of the images in this book illustrate individuals who are models. The depictions do not imply actual situations or events.

Cataloging-in-Publication Data

Names: McAneney, Caitie.
Title: What is a panic attack? / Caitie McAneney.
Description: New York : PowerKids Press, 2021. | Series: Understanding anxiety | Includes glossary and index.
Identifiers: ISBN 9781725318014 (pbk.) | ISBN 9781725318038 (library bound) | ISBN 9781725318021 (6 pack)
Subjects: LCSH: Anxiety–Juvenile literature. | Anxiety disorders–Juvenile literature. | Panic disorders–Treatment–Juvenile literature.
Classification: LCC BF723.A5 M38 2021 | DDC 155.4'18232–dc23

Manufactured in the United States of America

CPSIA Compliance Information: Batch #CSPK20. For Further Information contact Rosen Publishing, New York, New York at 1-800-237-9932.

Find us on

CONTENTS

PANIC ATTACK! 4
WHAT IS A PANIC ATTACK? 6
WHY PANIC? 8
THE MIND TAKES OVER 10
A RUSH 12
GETTING HELP 14
AVOIDING THE PANIC 16
KEEPING CALM 18
HELPING OTHERS 20
YOU'RE IN CONTROL 22
GLOSSARY 23
INDEX 24
WEBSITES 24

PANIC ATTACK!

Imagine you're on an airplane. You've never flown before, and you're a little nervous. You look out the window. All of a sudden, you panic! Your heart pounds. Your throat gets tight. Your mind races. You feel like you're losing control!

This is a panic attack. Even though you're safe, your mind and body are ready to fight or run away. That's because they think there is a **threat**. It can be very scary. However, panic attacks aren't uncommon.

Panic attacks can make you feel like you're in great danger. However, you're most likely safe.

WHAT IS A PANIC ATTACK?

A panic attack is a sudden **episode** of great anxiety, or fear. It's a strong physical, or bodily, **reaction**. Panic can't hurt you, but it can be very upsetting. What does it feel like?

Your heart might beat very quickly and strongly. Your stomach or head might hurt, or you could feel dizzy. It might be hard to breathe or swallow. Your thoughts might spin out of control. All of these feelings can be very scary!

KNOWING THE SIGNS OF A PANIC ATTACK CAN HELP YOU NAME IT AND DEAL WITH IT.

WHY PANIC?

The best way to beat anxiety is to understand it. So why do panic attacks happen?

There's a reason for anxiety and fear—to keep you safe. It's good to be afraid of deadly animals, for example. But our brains can react to things that aren't harmful, too, like speaking in public or flying in an airplane. This is called the fight-or-flight **response**. It's your body's way of getting you ready to fight a threat or run away from it, keeping you safe.

THE FIGHT-OR-FLIGHT RESPONSE WAS IMPORTANT FOR OUR **ANCESTORS**. THOUSANDS OF YEARS AGO, IT KEPT THEM SAFE FROM WILD ANIMALS!

THE MIND TAKES OVER

What goes through your mind during a panic attack? Many people feel like they're losing control. Thoughts move quickly. Many of them are scary. Examples are: What if I'm having a heart attack? What if I'm stuck on this bus for hours? What if I mess up in front of my whole class?

Some people say having a panic attack makes them feel like they're going crazy. They have trouble paying attention to things. They can only **focus** on the strong feelings in their body.

Racing thoughts may seem impossible to control. It might feel like they're taking over your mind.

A RUSH

You might feel like panic is taking over your body during a panic attack. A **chemical** in your body called **adrenaline** gets it ready to fight, flight, or even freeze—stopping in your tracks.

Adrenaline makes the heart beat very fast. It sends a rush of blood to important muscles in your legs or arms. Your lungs work quicker, too, making your breathing faster and harder. It might be hard to see. You might get the chills or start to sweat. That usually lasts two or three minutes.

ADRENALINE CAN HELP GIVE YOU MORE ENERGY TO PLAY SPORTS, BUT IT CAN WORK AGAINST YOU IN A PANIC ATTACK.

GETTING HELP

Panic attacks can make you feel alone, but you're not. There are many people to **support** you. Talking about your feelings can help you work through them. You can talk to a parent, teacher, or friend. You might even discover that other people you know have panic attacks, too.

You can also talk to a mental, or mind, health **professional**. This might be someone called a counselor or psychologist. They can help you control your feelings. Talking about your problems sometimes helps you get better. But sometimes, doctors might give you medicine, or drugs.

> TALK TO A TRUSTED ADULT ABOUT YOUR PANIC ATTACKS. THEY CAN HELP YOU CALM DOWN AND FEEL SAFE.

15

AVOIDING THE PANIC

Imagine you have a panic attack on a bus. You might start to avoid that bus or all buses. You don't want to go to the place where it happened. That makes you even more anxious.

Avoiding certain places or things is common for people who have panic attacks. If you don't go on the bus, then you're safe. Right? However, avoiding things often makes anxiety worse. The more panic attacks you have, the fewer places you'll be comfortable in, and the smaller your world can become.

A GOOD THING YOU CAN DO IS VISIT THE PLACE OR ACTIVITY THAT SCARES YOU. IT HELPS YOU REALIZE THAT IT'S PERFECTLY SAFE!

KEEPING CALM

The good thing about panic attacks is that they don't last forever. They can't hurt you. In time, the adrenaline will stop, and the panic attack will end.

You can become calm faster by breathing differently. Take deep, slow "belly breaths," feeling your belly rise and fall. Relax, or loosen, the parts of your body that feel tight. Keep your mind busy by saying the alphabet. This will tell your brain that there's no threat, and it can calm down.

> WHEN YOU'RE HAVING A PANIC ATTACK, ASK YOURSELF WHAT YOU SEE, HEAR, SMELL, TASTE, AND FEEL. THAT WILL KEEP YOU IN THE PRESENT MOMENT AND LOWER YOUR PANIC LEVELS.

HELPING OTHERS

Maybe you've never had a panic attack. But you have a friend who might be having one. What can you do to help?

First, be calm and respectful. Let them know that what they're feeling is OK. They don't have to feel **embarrassed**. Help your friend breathe slowly and deeply. You can count as they breathe—in for four seconds, out for eight. Help them focus on the present moment by getting them cold water or rubbing their back.

A GOOD FRIEND IS A GREAT HELP TO SOMEONE WHO'S HAVING A PANIC ATTACK!

YOU'RE IN CONTROL

Panic attacks often feel like a total loss of control. You might think you can't do anything to get better! Focus on what you *can* do in that moment. You can breathe. You can think about the present. You can wait until the rush of adrenaline passes.

Panic attacks keep some people from doing things they love, such as traveling, performing on stage, or playing a sport. But they don't have to do this. Remember you are stronger than your feelings. You are in control.

GLOSSARY

adrenaline: A matter that's part of the body's response to strong emotion.
ancestor: Someone who has come before you in a family line.
chemical: Matter that can be mixed with other matter to cause changes.
embarrassed: Feeling or showing awareness for something you feel you've done wrong.
episode: A short event that happens.
focus: To pay lots of attention to a task or event.
professional: Someone who does something for a living.
reaction: Acting a certain way because of something.
response: Saying or doing something in return.
support: To be there for others in a time of need, with helpful words or actions.
threat: Something that might hurt you.

INDEX

A
adrenaline, 12, 13, 18, 22
anxiety, 6, 8, 16

B
blood, 12
body, 4, 8, 10, 18
brain, 8, 18

C
chemical, 12
counselor, 14

D
danger, 5

F
fear, 6, 8
feelings, 6, 10, 14, 22
fight-or-flight response, 8, 9

H
head, 6
heart, 4, 6, 10, 12

L
lungs, 12

M
medicine, 14
mind, 4, 11, 14, 18
muscles, 12

P
psychologist, 14

S
stomach, 6

T
thoughts, 6, 11
threat, 4, 8
throat, 4

WEBSITES

Due to the changing nature of Internet links, PowerKids Press has developed an online list of websites related to the subject of this book. This site is updated regularly. Please use this link to access the list: www.powerkidslinks.com/ua/panicattack